Agent 41

Daniel Pluck

MW01609040

illustrated by Brent Putze

Learning Media®

Pssst! Don't tell anyone, but I'm an undercover agent. I collect important information that is used to save lives all over the country.

Each day, I'm given a mission. I never know where my mission is going to take me. Like every good agent, I'm prepared for anything.

Today, my mission will take me into the middle of the city. I start the day with peanut butter and jelly on toast. I dress carefully so that I won't stand out. Before I leave, I put on a cap to protect me and hide my face.

3

I'm more than a little nervous as I report for duty at Spy Central. I'm told where my mission will be and given my spy gadget. I carefully exit the building in disguise. It's important that I'm not recognized. I've been trained in cover-up techniques. Looking casual, I study my notebook and whistle a little tune. My spy gadget has been cleverly designed to fit into my pocket. I keep it hidden at all times, using it without anyone noticing.

Spying is not an easy job. It can be boring, but you must stay alert at all times. I stand on the sidewalk all day, breathing exhaust fumes. As I look into the faces of the people passing by, I can see their questioning looks. There is no time for chitchat, so I just smile and look away.

Oops! Emergency! Some of my friends are across the road. I dive behind a mailbox, but it's too late. They see me and wave. They could blow my cover and distract me from my mission. I nod, give a brief smile, and focus back on my work.

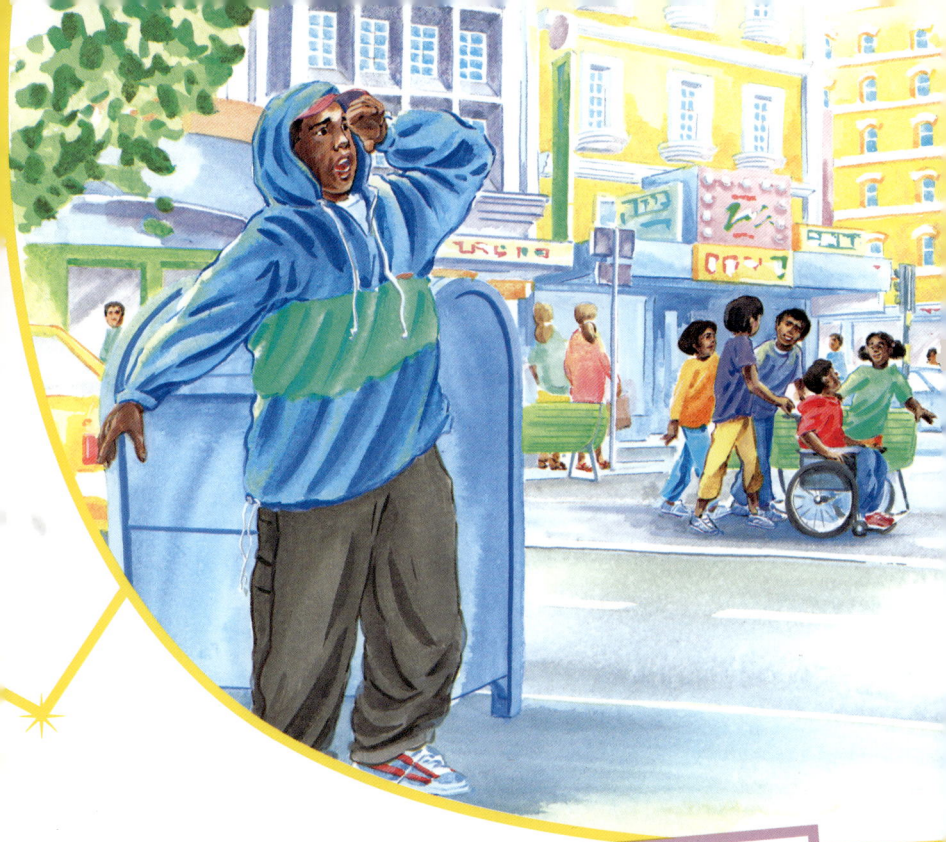

Now that I've been seen, I'm forced to make an urgent decision. Do I stay and risk the mission, or do I pull out and move on? My friends are moving off down the street, so I decide to stay. It was a close call, but the coast is now clear. My mission is safe.

The day is coming to an end, so I collect the last of the data and retire. Back at Spy Central, I sign in and pass on the information.

"A few close calls out there today, boss. I counted 3,017 cars, and sixty-seven people weren't wearing seat belts. I'll live to see another day, but those people may not. Thanks – this has been a great holiday job. This is Agent 41 checking out."